Year 3
Workbook

Pearson

Published by Pearson Education Limited, 80 Strand, London, WC2R 0RL.

www.pearson.com/international-schools

Copies of official specifications for all Pearson Edexcel qualifications may be found on the website: https://qualifications.pearson.com

Text © Pearson Education Limited 2023
Produced by Just Content Ltd
Designed by PDQ Media Digital Media Solutions
Typeset by PDQ Media Digital Media Solutions
Picture research by Straive Ltd
Original illustrations © Pearson Education Limited 2023
Cover design © Pearson Education Limited 2023

The right of Lesley Butcher to be identified as the author of this work has been asserted by her in accordance with the Copyright, Designs and Patents Act 1988.

First published 2023

26 25 24
10 9 8 7

British Library Cataloguing in Publication Data
A catalogue record for this book is available from the British Library

ISBN 978 1 292 43325 7

Printed in the UK by Bell & Bain

Animal adaptations

There are many different types of habitat around the world. Some animals are adapted to live in Arctic snow. Others are adapted to live in warm, wet rainforests.

In this unit we will learn:

- to group animals
- to use a key to identify animals
- to describe ways in which animals are suited to their habitat
- how to compare animals in contrasting habitats
- to predict the habitat of some animals by looking at their adaptations.

Giant tortoises like me can live for more than 100 years. We eat grass, leaves and cactus plants. We can store lots of water to help us to survive in dry habitats.
I have dry scales on my legs. Which animal group do I belong to?

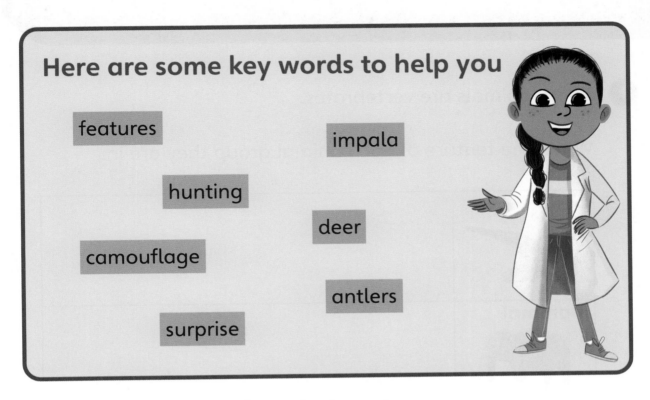

Here are some key words to help you

features

impala

hunting

deer

camouflage

antlers

surprise

Choose two key words from the box above.
Write or draw what they mean.

Grouping animals

1 These animals are vertebrates.

Write **one** feature of each animal group they are in.

bird	
mammal	
amphibian	
reptile	
fish	

2 a) What name do we give to animals **without** a backbone?

_____

b) Write **one** feature of each group these animals are in.

insects	
spiders	
crustaceans	
worms	
starfish	
molluscs	

c) Name **two** other animals that are **molluscs**.

1. _____

2. _____

Identifying animals

1. Put a tick (✓) or a cross (✗) to describe the features of each animal.

   One has been done for you.

	vertebrate?	feathers?	hump on back?	pincers?	wings?
flamingo	✓	✓	✗	✗	✓
lobster					
camel					
giraffe					
slug					
moth					

2 Use the key to write letter **A**, **B**, **C**, **D**, **E** or **F** under each animal picture.

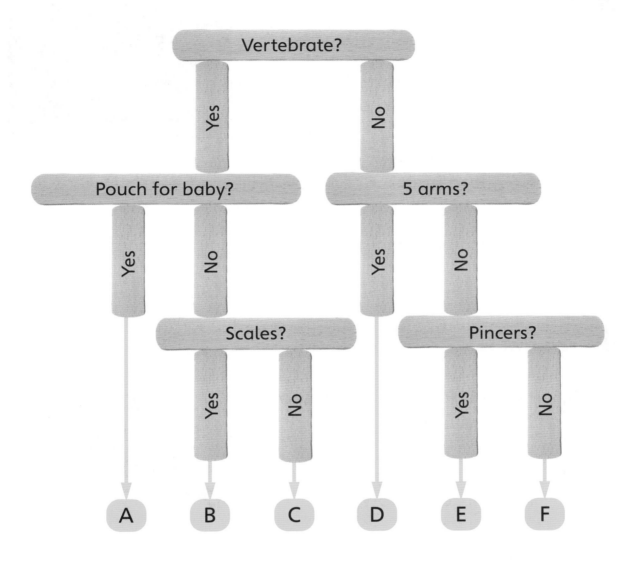

Vertebrate?

Yes — No

Pouch for baby?   5 arms?

Yes — No   Yes — No

Scales?   Pincers?

Yes — No   Yes — No

A   B   C   D   E   F

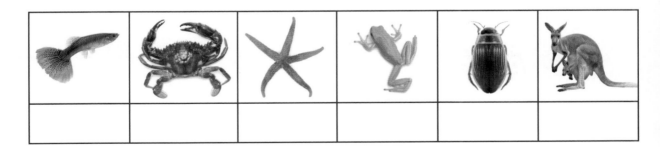

Owls

1 a)   Label the feathers on this owl's head.

   b)   Label **one** feature that shows it is a bird of prey.

   c)   How do the owl's eyes help it to hunt?

   _____

   _____

2 This owl sees an animal to eat.

   a)   Label **one** feature that shows this owl is a bird of prey.

   b)   Label something that helps it to fly slowly.

   c)   Why does the animal **not** hear the owl coming?

   _____

   _____

   d)   What does *camouflage* mean?

   _____

3 Draw a barn owl using the outline below.

barn owl

a) Draw its **face**, **eyes** and **curved beak**.

b) Draw another **leg**.

Each **foot** has **four toes** with **four talons**.

c) Draw and colour some **feathers** on its body.

Impala

1. Circle **two** animal groups that an impala is grouped in.

   crustaceans   molluscs   reptiles

   invertebrates   mammals   birds   vertebrates

2. a)   Why do impala live in herds?

   _____

   b)   Impala can run very fast and jump.

   (i)   Which life process is this? _____

   (ii)   Why do impala need to run very fast?

   _____

   (iii) What do they jump over? _____

3. a)   Which impala have horns? _____

   b)   What do these impala do with their horns?

   _____

4. Some animals have antlers that do the same job as horns.

   a)   Name an animal that has antlers.

   _____

b) Draw one line from each animal to the one with the most similar horns or antlers.

Making a snail habitat

1 Circle **two** animal groups that a snail is grouped in.

invertebrates   crustaceans   vertebrates

molluscs   reptiles   mammals   birds

2 a) Some snails live on land.
Circle **two** words to describe their habitat.

hot   damp   snowy   dry   shady

b) Name **two** other places some snails can live.

1. _____

2. _____

3 Class 3 make a snail habitat in a tank.

a) Why does the tank need a lid?

_____

b) Why does the lid need to have small holes in it?

_____

c) Why do they need to mist the tank with water?

_____

d)   Why do they keep the tank away from sunlight?

_____

4 a)   Draw a habitat in this tank that you think a land snail would like to live in.

Label the things you draw.

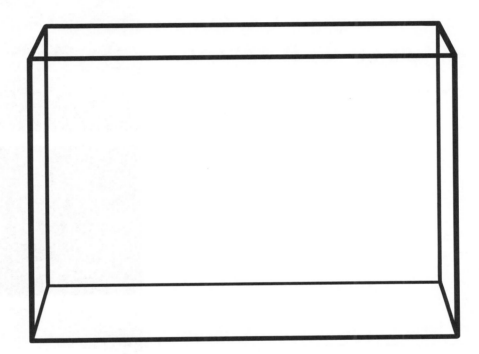

b)   Write **two** things you will change regularly in your tank.

1. _____

2. _____

The habitat game

1 Draw **one** line from each animal to its habitat.

camel

parrot

shark

polar bear

lion

2 a) Name a type of habitat near the place where you live.

_____

b) Draw an animal that lives there with the habitat around it.

Name of animal: _____

```



```

c) Find out what your animal eats and what it lives in.

_____

_____

_____

_____

What have I learned?

1 I can group animals using features that I observe.

I can also use a key to identify animals.

I know this because I know that animals with **backbones** are grouped as _____.

Animals with **scaly skin** are grouped as

_____.

Animals with **three body parts** called head, thorax and abdomen are grouped as _____.

2 I can describe ways in which animals are suited to their habitat.

I know this because I can write **one** adaptation of each of these animals:

Polar bear _____

Camel _____

Owl _____

3 I can compare animals in contrasting habitats.

I know this because I can describe the habitat of:

A snail _____

A polar bear _____

I can also describe a habitat near where I live.

_____

4 I can predict the habitat of some animals by looking at their adaptations.

I know this because I can predict the habitat of these two animals by describing their fur and their ears.

Habitat: _____   _____

Fur: _____   _____

Ears: _____   _____

Teeth

Human teeth are not all the same size or shape. We use some teeth to bite and some to chew. Animals have different types of teeth to suit their diet.

In this unit we will learn:

- that human teeth are not all the same size or shape
- the main types of human teeth
- how to link the shape of a tooth to its function
- that teeth are part of the digestive system
- how to compare types of teeth in different animals
- the meaning of 'herbivore', 'omnivore' and 'carnivore'.

Have you noticed that your teeth are not all the same shape? Some are shaped for biting and others are shaped for chewing. I have some of my adult teeth now. They are bigger than my other teeth. Do you have any of your adult teeth?

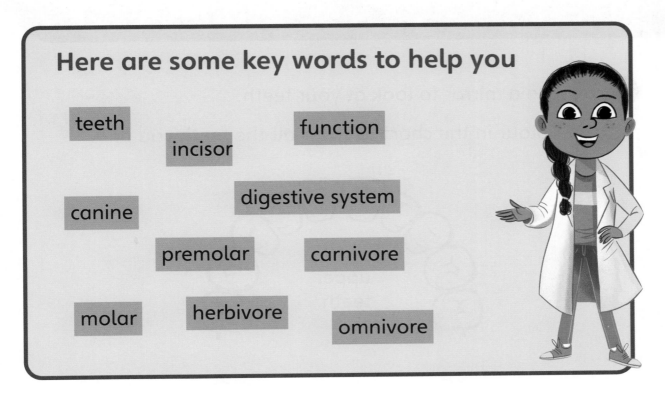

Here are some key words to help you

teeth

incisor

function

canine

digestive system

premolar

carnivore

molar

herbivore

omnivore

Choose two key words from the box above.
Write or draw what they mean.

Looking at our teeth

1 a) Use a mirror to look at your teeth.

Colour in the chart to show all the teeth you find.

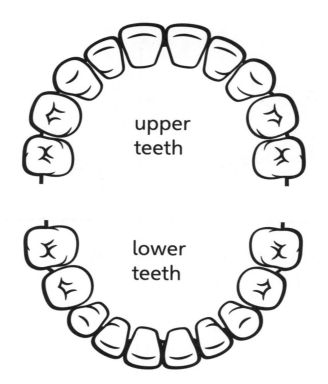

b) Do you have any missing teeth? How many?

_____

c) Do you have any adult teeth starting to grow yet?

Where in your mouth are they?

_____

d) How many teeth do you have altogether?

2 At different ages, children's first teeth fall out.
Adult teeth grow in their place.

The table shows the age at which the numbered teeth on the diagram start to change.

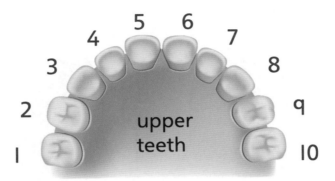

Age of children in years	Upper teeth that change
6 to 8	5 and 6
7 to 8	4 and 7
10 to 12	3 and 8
9 to 11	2 and 9
10 to 12	1 and 10

Use the **purple** tooth numbers from the diagram and right column in the table to answer parts a) and b).

a) Which **two** teeth change first? ☐ ☐

b) Which **four** teeth change last?

☐ ☐ ☐ ☐

c) At what age do teeth first start changing? _____

d) In which part of the upper mouth do teeth change first?

_____

Different shaped teeth

1 Draw a line from each word to label the tooth.

crown

root

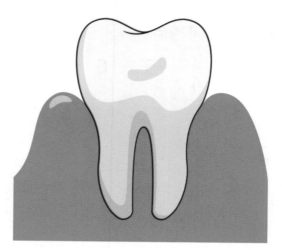

gum

2 Draw **one** line from each diagram to match teeth that are the same.

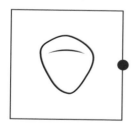

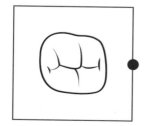

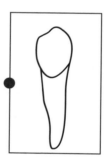

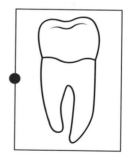

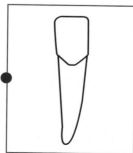

3 The diagrams show the teeth of a child and the teeth of an adult.

_____   _____

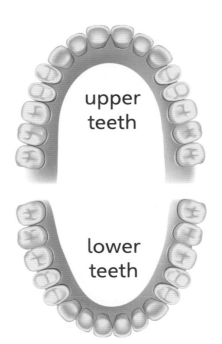

a) Write a title above each diagram.

b) Count how many teeth each diagram shows.

The adult has ☐ teeth.

The child has ☐ teeth.

c) Label an **incisor** tooth on each diagram.

d) Label a **molar** tooth on each diagram.

e) Name the other **two** types of human teeth.

1. _____   2. _____

Functions of teeth

1   Write another word that means *function*.

2   a)   Name each type of tooth.

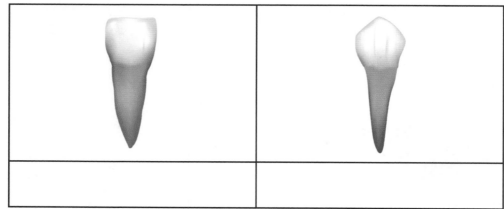

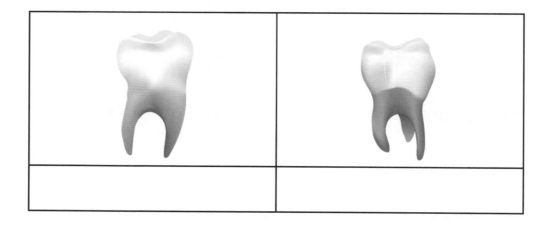

b)   Label the **two** different parts of this tooth. Use a line and a word each time.

3 a) Write **upper teeth** and **lower teeth** on the diagram.

b) Name each of the coloured teeth in the table

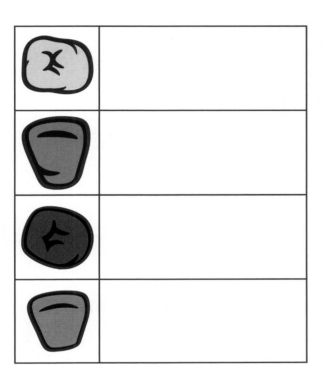

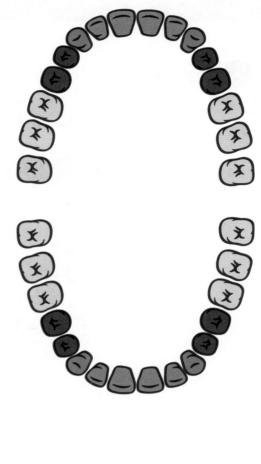

c) (i) Circle the **two** types of teeth used for chewing.

(ii) What are the teeth you have **not** circled used to do?

_____

d) Name the type of tooth that is used to grind food.

_____

Why do we need teeth?

1 a) Draw a line from each word to label the diagram.

incisor tooth

tongue

molar tooth

lip

b) Food goes down a hole at the back of the mouth.

Write **one** word to describe this. _____

c) Which life process is eating food? _____

d) Complete the sentences.

Our teeth are _____ our mouths.

Our mouths are the start of our _____
system.

e) What does the word *system* mean here?

_____

2 a)   What do teeth do when we put food into our mouth?

   _____

   b)   What does our tongue do to the food?

   _____

   c)   (i)   Circle **one** word that describes saliva.

                green   hard   rough   wet

         (ii)   What does saliva do to food?

                _____

3 What does the digestive system do to our food?

   _____

   _____

   _____

   _____

   _____

Comparing teeth

1 a)   How many different types of teeth do adult humans have?

☐

b)   Write the names of the different types of human teeth.

_____

_____

2 Write **yes** or **no** in each row of the table about birds.

Do birds have...	Yes or no?
wings?	
teeth?	
feathers?	
a tongue?	

3 Write **yes** or **no** in each row of the table about tortoises.

Do tortoises have...	Yes or no?
teeth?	
hard jaws?	
a tongue?	

4 This crocodile is eating a fish.

a) Draw the shape of one of the crocodile's teeth.

b) What is it using its teeth to do? Circle **one** answer.

hold the fish   chew the fish

wet the fish   smell the fish

c) How do crocodile teeth differ from human teeth?

_____

_____

_____

d) Write **one** feature that shows the crocodile is a reptile.

_____

Carnivores

1 a) What do carnivores eat?

_____

b) Circle the tiger that is living **in the wild**.

c) Describe what this tiger is doing and why.

tiger   **bird**

What the tiger is doing:

_____

_____

Why the tiger is doing this:

_____

_____

d)   Circle **two** words that best describe the tiger's teeth.

  slow   snowy   sharp   soft   strong

2   The diagram shows four types of carnivore teeth.
Each type of tooth is a different colour.

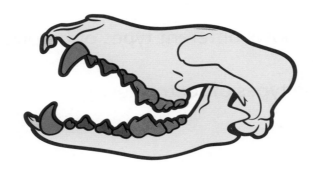

a)   Name the four types of teeth shown.

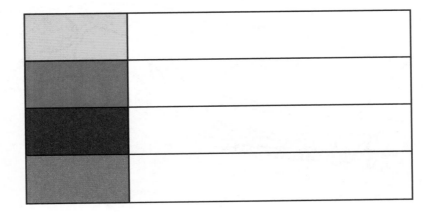

b)   What does this carnivore use these teeth for?

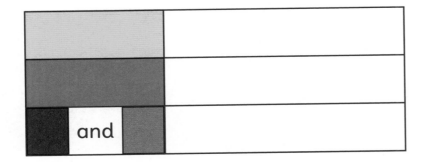

Herbivores

1. a) What do herbivores eat? _____

   b) Why do herbivores **not** need to run to catch food?

   _____

2. The diagram shows different types of herbivore teeth.

   a) Name the types of teeth shown.

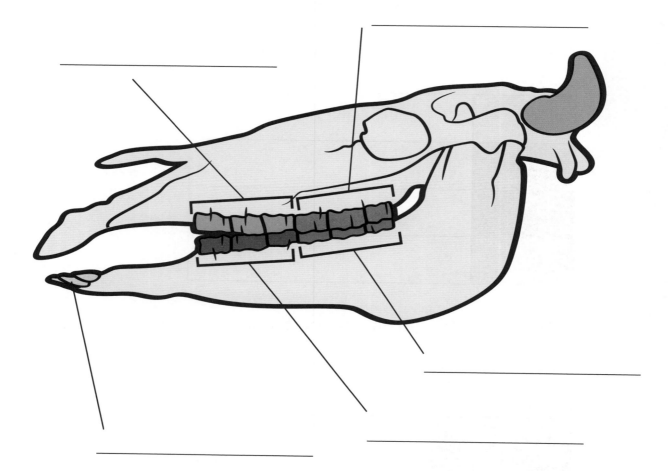

b) Name **one** type of tooth that this herbivore does **not** have.

_____

c) Name **one** type of tooth that this herbivore only has in its lower jaw.

_____

3 Complete the table to compare the teeth of the herbivore and the carnivore.

Put **one** tick (✓) in each row.

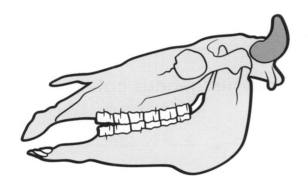

herbivore

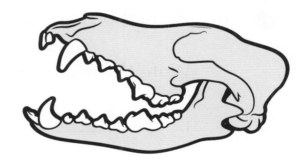

carnivore

	herbivore	carnivore
Which has sharper teeth?		
Which has long canines?		
Which has ridges on its molars?		
Which has a hard pad of gum instead of teeth?		
Which has a big space between front and back teeth?		

Omnivores

1 a)   What do herbivores eat? _____

b)   What do carnivores eat? _____

c)   What do omnivores eat?

_____

d)   Circle the word that describes humans.

herbivore   carnivore   omnivore

2 a)   Hedgehogs are omnivores.

Write **three** different things that hedgehogs eat.

1. _____   2. _____

3. _____

b)   Raccoons are omnivores.

Write **two** different things that raccoons eat.

1. _____   2. _____

c)   (i)   Which of the foods you listed in a) and b)
are **plants**?

_____

(ii)   Which of the foods you listed in a) and b) are **animals**?

_____

3 a)   What parts of plants do long-tailed macaques eat?

_____

b)   What other food do they eat that shows they are omnivores?

_____

4 This capuchin monkey is an omnivore. Look at its teeth.

a)   Label **one incisor** tooth and **one canine** tooth.

b)   How do the monkey's canines differ from a tiger's canines?

_____

_____

What have I learned?

1 I know that human teeth are not all the same size or shape.

I know this because humans have _____ different types of teeth.

2 I can identify and name the main types of human teeth.

I know this because I can name these teeth:

_____   _____   _____   _____

3 I can link the shape of a tooth to its function.

I know this because I can complete these words that describe what teeth do.

Sl_____   **Te**_____   **Gr**_____

Humans use teeth at the front to **bi**_____ and teeth at

the back to **ch**_____ food.

4 I know that teeth are part of the _____ system.

I know that teeth break down food into pieces so we can

_____ it.

5 I can compare types of teeth in different animals.

I know this because I can draw a crocodile tooth and an iguana tooth here.

crocodile tooth	iguana tooth

6 I know the meaning of **herbivore**, **omnivore** and **carnivore**.

I can identify them from their diet and by looking at their teeth.

Herbivores only eat _____.

They have _____ on their back teeth to

_____ plants.

Omnivores eat _____.

They have teeth of different shapes and sizes like ours.

Carnivores only eat _____.

They have very sharp teeth and long

_____ teeth.

Feeding relationships

Every animal needs food to survive. Plants make their own food, but animals depend on plants or other animals for food. We can show the relationship between plants and animals using food chains.

In this unit we will learn:

- that living things need food
- that food supply affects an animal population
- how to use the words 'producer', 'consumer', 'predator' and 'prey'
- how to draw and interpret food chains
- that plants make their own food, but animals depend on plants and/or other animals as a food source
- how to identify a producer, consumer, herbivore, predator and prey in food chains and food webs.

Whenever I see something good to eat, I swoop down and catch it. I like fish and crabs best but sometimes I see humans eating something nice and I try to taste it too. Have you seen gulls like me looking for food where you live?

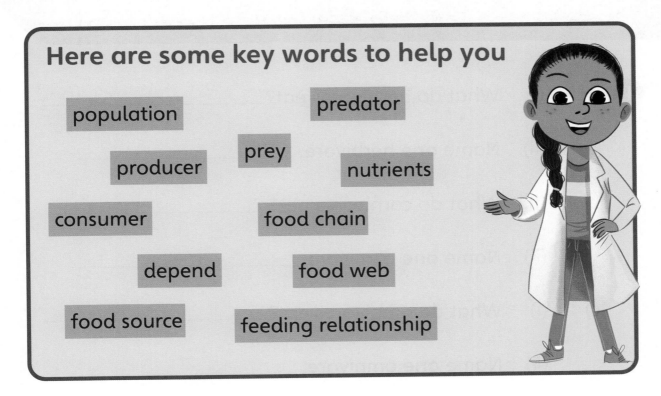

Here are some key words to help you

population

predator

prey

producer

nutrients

consumer

food chain

depend

food web

food source

feeding relationship

Choose two key words from the box above.
Write or draw what they mean.

Animals need food

1 a)   (i)   What do herbivores eat? _____

           (ii)   Name **one** herbivore. _____

   b)   (i)   What do carnivores eat? _____

           (ii)   Name **one** carnivore. _____

   c)   (i)   What do omnivores eat? _____

           (ii)   Name **one** omnivore. _____

2 a)   Which life process is eating food?

       _____

   b)   What happens to an animal if it cannot get any food?

       _____

3 Complete the sentence.

In the wild, all the living things of the

same _____ who live in the

same _____ are called

a _____ .

4 a)   Name the animals in this picture.

_____

b)   What do these animals eat?

_____

c)   Fish eat tiny plants, tiny animals or both.

Predict what happens to a big fish population if there
are **not enough** tiny plants and animals to eat.

_____

d)   Predict what happens to a big penguin population if
there are not enough fish.

_____

e)   Which of these may happen if there is not enough **food**
for the penguins?

Tick (✓) **one** answer.

The penguins have more babies.   ☐

Lots of baby penguins die.   ☐

Adult penguins grow fatter.   ☐

Penguins start to make their own food.   ☐

Producers and consumers

1   a)   Label the part of this plant that makes its food. Use a word and a line.

b)   Circle the living thing that is most likely to eat this plant.

| A | B | C | D |

c)   Use the letters under the pictures above to answer these questions.

(i)   Which living thing makes its own food? _____

(ii)   Which living things eat other animals? _____

(iii)   Which living things are consumers? _____

d)   Write one scientific word for living things that make their own food.

_____

2 Write the scientific name for each of these diet groups and name an animal with this diet.

Animals that **only** eat **plants** are _____.

Name of an animal with this diet: _____

Animals that **only** eat **other animals** are

_____.

Name of an animal with this diet: _____

Animals that **eat plants and other animals** are

_____.

Name of an animal with this diet: _____

3 Label **producer** and **consumer** in both pictures.
Use label lines and the words.

Animal food sources

1 a) Circle the plant.

| thrush | banana tree | snail | frog |

b) Name **one** producer in the pictures.

_____

c) Name **one** consumer in the pictures.

_____

d) Snails only eat plants.

Circle the word that describes a snail's diet.

carnivore   omnivore   herbivore

e) Frogs only eat animals like insects and worms.

Circle the word that describes a frog's diet.

carnivore   omnivore   herbivore

2 For this question, use information from question 1 as well as your textbook.

a) What do frogs depend on as a food source?

_____

b) What do snails depend on as a food source?

_____

c) What do snakes depend on as a food source?

_____

d) What do grasshoppers depend on as a food source?

_____

3 a) What do plants need to make their own food?

_____

b) (i) Name **two** producers that grow where you live.

1. _____ 2. _____

(ii) Name **two** consumers that depend on them.

1. _____ 2. _____

Predators

1 a) Complete the sentence.

A predator is an animal that _____,

_____ and _____ other

_____.

b) (i) Draw a **reptile** that is a predator. Write its name.

(ii) Draw a **mammal** that is a predator. Write its name.

(iii) Draw a different predator that lives near your school. Write its name.

2 a) Draw a predator and its prey.

b) Name the living things that you draw.

c) Write 'predator' and 'prey' beside the correct pictures.

3 Tick (✓) **one** correct statement in a) and **one** in b).

a) Predators can be animals or plants. ☐

Predators and prey are always plants. ☐

Prey can be animals or plants. ☐

Predators and prey are always animals. ☐

b) Predators are always herbivores. ☐

Carnivores are predators. ☐

The food that prey eat is called a predator. ☐

Herbivores can make their own food. ☐

1 a) Write **producer** or **consumer** under the name of each living thing.

Slugs eat marigold plants.

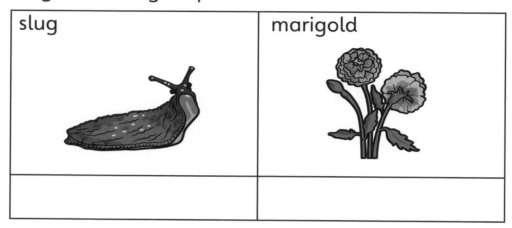

slug	marigold

Birds called thrushes eat slugs.

Birds of prey called sparrowhawks eat thrushes.

thrush	sparrowhawk

b) Put ticks (✓) in each row of the table.

Animal	Is it a predator?	Is it prey?
slug		
thrush		
sparrowhawk		

c)   80 marigold plants are growing in this field.

How many slugs are in the field? ☐

d)   Suggest how many thrushes could find enough food in this field. Circle your suggestion.

100   80   40   5

e)   Only one sparrowhawk feeds in this field.

What would happen if 20 sparrowhawks tried to feed in this field?

_____

_____

Food chains

1 Look at this food chain.

grass   rabbit   fox

a)   What do foxes eat? _____

b)   What do rabbits eat? _____

c)   Write **producer** or **consumer** under each name.

grass	rabbit	fox

d)   Write **predator** or **prey** under each name.

rabbit	fox

e)   How do producers get food?

_____

2 Snails eat lettuce plants.

snail   lettuce plant

Thrushes eat snails. Sparrowhawks eat thrushes.

thrush

sparrowhawk

a) Write a food chain for these four living things.

b) Name **one** producer. _____

c) Name **one** consumer. _____

d) Name **two** predators.

1. _____ 2. _____

e) Name **two** prey.

1. _____ 2. _____

f) What does the word *nutrients* mean?

_____

_____

More feeding relationships

1 a) Use the names of the living things in the pictures to complete the sentences.

mouse eating a plant

hawk eating a mouse

The _____ is a herbivore because it is

eating a _____.

The _____ is a producer because it can

make its own food.

The _____ is a carnivore because it is

eating a _____.

The _____ is a predator of the

_____.

The _____ is the prey of the

_____.

b) Write a food chain for the hawk, mouse and plant.

2 This is a small food web. Use it to answer the questions.

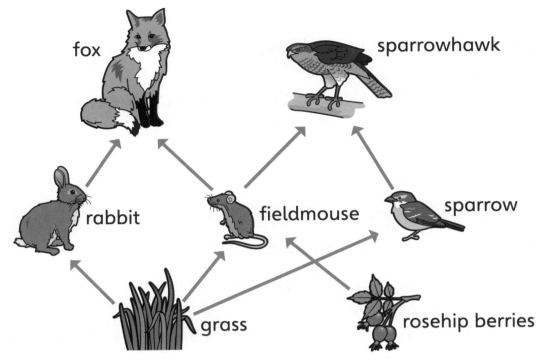

fox

sparrowhawk

rabbit

fieldmouse

sparrow

grass

rosehip berries

a) Name **two** producers.

1. _____ 2. _____

b) Name **two** living things that a fieldmouse eats.

1. _____ 2. _____

c) Name **two** predators of a fieldmouse.

1. _____ 2. _____

d) Name **two** carnivores.

1. _____ 2. _____

e) Name **two** herbivores.

1. _____ 2. _____

What have I learned?

1 I understand that living things need food.

I understand that the food supply affects the size of an animal population and where they can live.

I know this because animals need to find enough

_____ to stay alive.

For example, herbivores need enough

_____ to stay alive.

2 I understand how to use the words **producer**, **consumer**, **predator** and **prey** and how to interpret food chains.

I can look at the relationship between predators and prey.

I know this because I can use the correct words to describe living things in this food chain:

lettuce plant → snail → thrush → sparrowhawk

producer _____

consumers _____

predators _____

prey _____

3 I understand that plants make their own food, but animals depend on plants and/or other animals as a food source. I can draw simple food chains to show this.

I know this because I can draw a food chain that shows a producer and three animals.

4 I can identify a **producer**, **consumer**, **herbivore**, **predator** and **prey** in a food web.

I know this because I can write each of the bold words **once** on this food web.

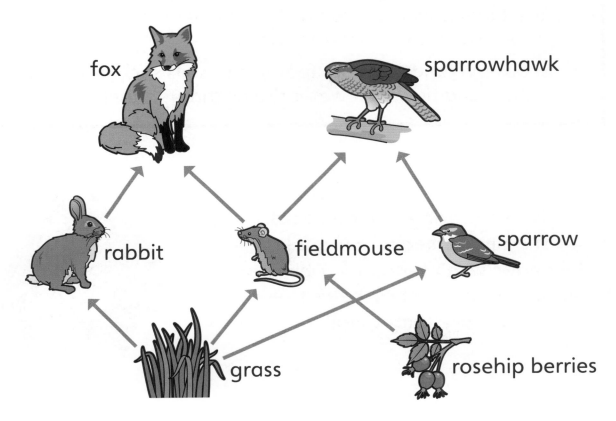

Rocks and soils

Inside the Earth it is so hot that rocks melt. But the outer layer of the Earth has solid rocks of different colours and textures. Rocks are often covered in soil.

In this unit we will learn:

- that different rocks have different properties and features
- to identify different rocks by observing them, by using a key and by finding things out for ourselves
- to describe how sedimentary, igneous and metamorphic rocks are formed
- to explain how rocks can be broken down into smaller pieces over time in different ways
- to observe and compare features of soils such as colour, texture and how well water drains through them.

I like sheltering behind rocks. The shade keeps me cool. I wonder what types of rock are near me? Have they been there a very long time?

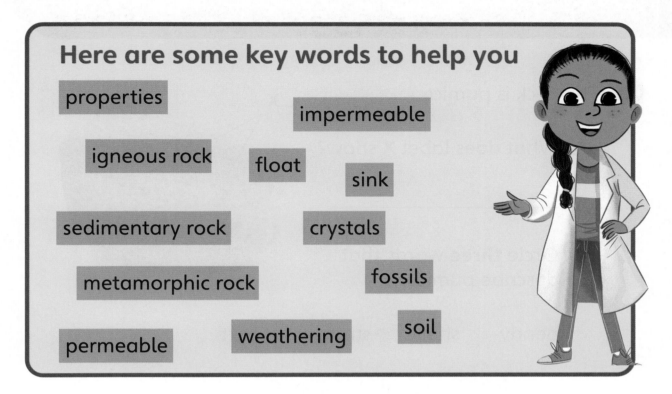

Here are some key words to help you

properties

impermeable

igneous rock

float

sink

sedimentary rock

crystals

metamorphic rock

fossils

permeable

weathering

soil

Choose two key words from the box above.
Write or draw what they mean.

A first look at rocks

1. This rock is pumice.

   a) What does label **X** show?

      _____

   b) Circle **three** words that describe pumice.

      bendy   shiny   stretchy   soft

      light   rough   smooth

   c) Describe **one** use for pumice.

      _____

      _____

2. This rock is granite.

   a) Circle **two** words that describe granite.

      bendy   hard   heavy   soft   light

b) Circle **two** words that describe granite after it has been polished.

stretchy   bendy   shiny   smooth   black

c) Write **one** use for granite.

_____

3 This rock is slate.

a) Draw **one** use for slate.

Write a sentence to say what your drawing shows.

_____

_____

b) Describe what slate is like.

_____

_____

Properties of rocks

1. Test some rocks to see if they are hard or soft.

   a) Complete the table by writing **Yes** or **No** on each row.

   There is space in the table to add another rock you test.

Type of rock	Can these objects scratch the rock?		
	fingernail	copper coin	steel nail
chalk			
limestone			
granite			
coal			

   b) (i) Which is the **hardest** rock you tested?

   _____

   (ii) How did you decide which rock is the hardest?

   _____

   c) (i) Which is the **softest** rock you tested?

   _____

   (ii) How did you decide which rock is the softest?

   _____

2 a) (i) What does *permeable* mean?

_____

(ii) Write a word that has the opposite meaning to

permeable. _____

b) Test some rocks to see if they are permeable.
Complete the table with your results.

Type of rock	What happens to drops of water on the rock?	Is the rock permeable?
pumice		
sandstone		
slate		
limestone		

3 Test some rocks to see if they float or sink in water.

a) Complete the table with your results.

Type of rock	Does it float or sink?
pumice	
granite	
slate	

b) Describe the properties of rock that floats.

_____

Using a key to identify rocks

1 Use the key to write letter **A**, **B**, **C**, **D** or **E** under each rock.

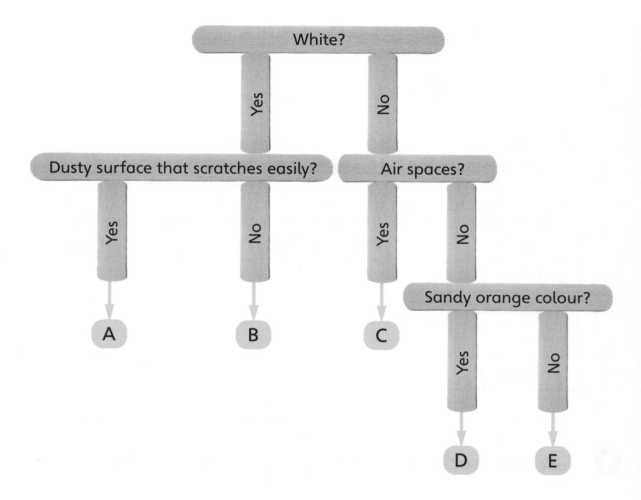

White?
- Yes
- No

Dusty surface that scratches easily?
- Yes → A
- No → B

Air spaces?
- Yes → C
- No

Sandy orange colour?
- Yes → D
- No → E

2 Use the key to write letter **P**, **Q**, **R**, **S** or **T** under each rock.

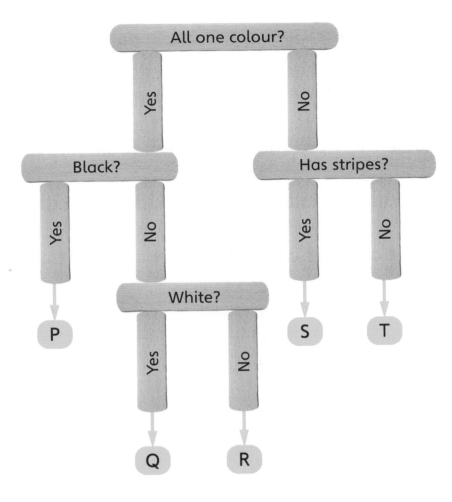

All one colour?
Yes — Black?
No — Has stripes?

Black?
Yes → P
No — White?

Has stripes?
Yes → S
No → T

White?
Yes → Q
No → R

Igneous rock

1 a) Which place has harder rocks? Circle your answer.

Earth's surface   deep inside the Earth

b) Circle the word that means *hot molten rock*.

igneous   volcano   shiny   magma   hard

c) Circle another word for *molten*.

wet   smelly   melted   cooled   stiff

2 Name **two** types of igneous rock.

1. _____

2. _____

3 Write **quickly** or **slowly** in the spaces.

When magma cools deep inside the Earth,
it cools _____.

Large crystals form when magma
cools _____.

When magma cools near the surface of the Earth,
it cools _____.

Smaller crystals form when magma cools _____.

4 Describe what you can see happening in this picture.

Label the picture if that helps you to describe it.

_____

_____

_____

_____

_____

Sedimentary rock

1 Draw **one** line from each sedimentary rock to its name.

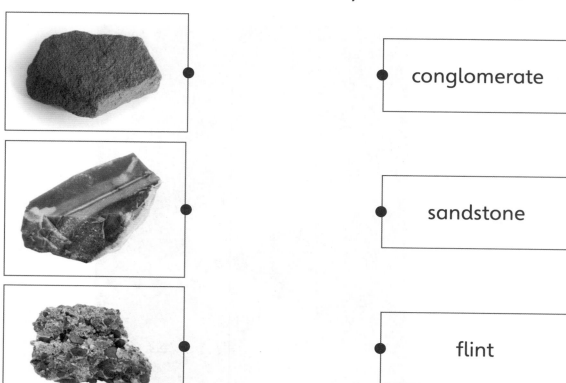

conglomerate

sandstone

flint

2 Circle all the pictures that show sedimentary rock.

3 The pictures show how sedimentary rock is made.

Write one or two sentences next to each picture to describe what is happening.

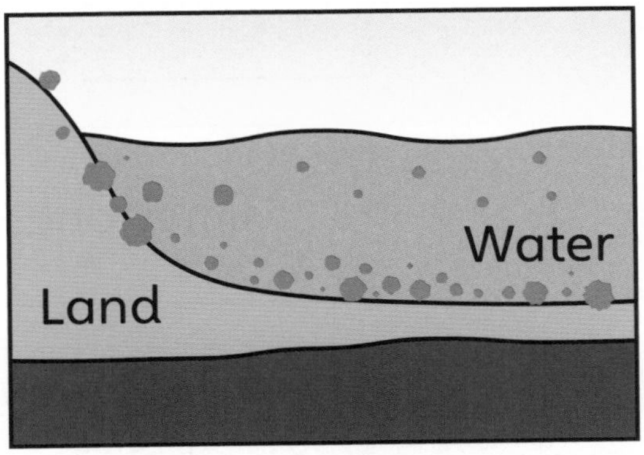

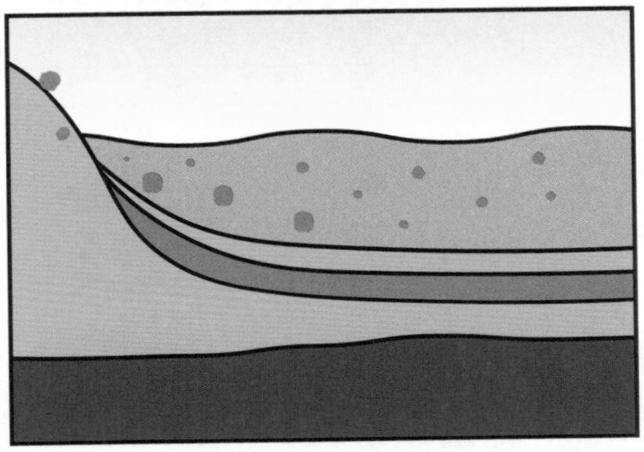

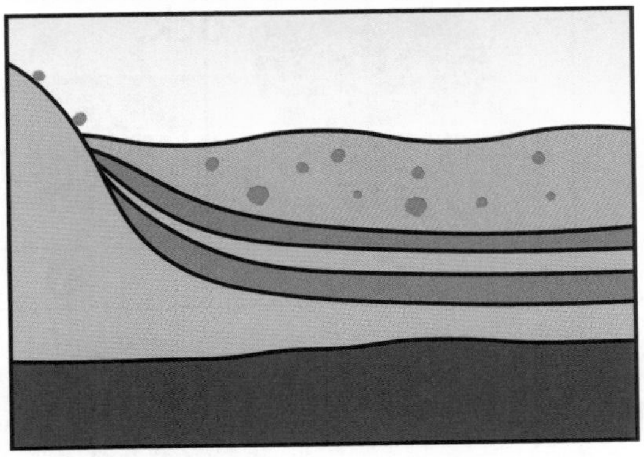

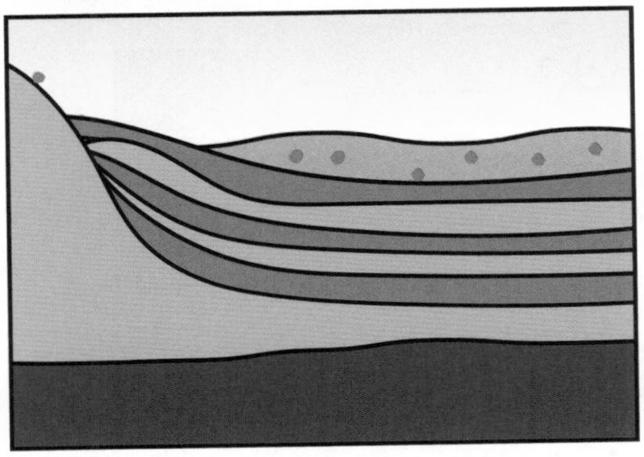

Land   Water

_____

_____

_____

_____

_____

_____

_____

_____

_____

_____

_____

_____

_____

_____

_____

_____

_____

_____

_____

_____

_____

_____

_____

Metamorphic rock

1 a) Draw **one** line from each rock to its name.

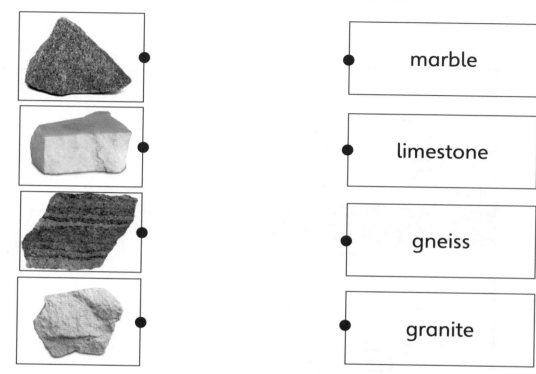

- marble
- limestone
- gneiss
- granite

b) Write letters on the lines to answer the questions.

| A | B | C | D |

(i) Which two are metamorphic rocks? _____ and _____

(ii) Which is a sedimentary rock? _____

(iii) Which is an igneous rock? _____

(iv) Which rock turns into marble? _____

(v) Which rock turns into gneiss? _____

2 a) Which **two** types of rock can change into metamorphic rock?

    1. _____   2. _____

   b) Which **two** factors cause other rocks to change to metamorphic rock?

    1. _____   2. _____

   c) Describe how metamorphic rock is formed by writing about what is happening in this picture.
Label the picture if it helps you to describe it.

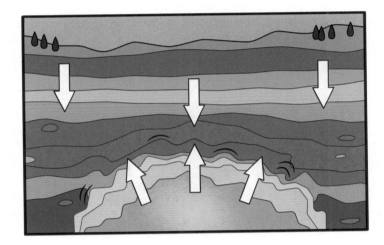

_____

_____

_____

_____

_____

_____

Fossils

1 Circle **one** answer in each part.

a) Which type of rock is limestone?

sedimentary   igneous   metamorphic

b) Which type of rock is made from layers of sediment?

metamorphic   sedimentary   igneous

2 A scientist finds this in an old rock.

a) What sort of living thing made this pattern?

_____

b) What do scientists call these patterns in rocks?

_____

c) Which type of rock is this most likely to be?

_____

3 a) What has happened to this dead fish?

_____

_____

b) (i) Name **one** part of this fish that was hard.

_____

(ii) Label this hard part on the picture.

(iii) Name **one** part of this fish that was softer.

_____

c) (i) What sort of habitat do fish live in?

_____

(ii) Suggest where this rock was found millions of

years ago. _____

d) Why are there no fish patterns like this in igneous rock?

_____

e) Suggest what the fish pattern might be like if this rock had changed to metamorphic rock.

_____

Weathering

1 a) Tick (✓) **one** thing that is happening to this rock.

It is getting bigger. ☐

It is changing into metamorphic rock. ☐

It is breaking into smaller pieces. ☐

It is changing colour. ☐

b) (i) How is weathering changing this rock?

_____

_____

(ii) Name **two** sorts of weather that can change rocks like this.

1. _____

2. _____

2 a) Which part of these plants is growing into cracks in the rock?

_____

b) What will happen to this rock?

_____

3 Write one sentence about each picture to describe what is happening.

Picture 1

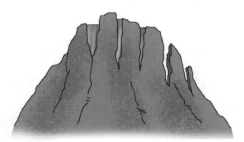

Picture 2

In Picture 1 _____

_____

In Picture 2 _____

_____

4 Describe how this sandstone rock has become mushroom shaped.

Write about the top part and then write about the bottom part.

_____

_____

_____

_____

_____

What is soil?

1. The picture shows a tree.

   a) Draw some soil in the picture to show which part of the tree is covered by soil.

   b) Name the part of a plant that is in the soil.

   _____

2. Complete the sentence.

   Soil is made from:

   • small parts of _____ called

   _____

   • _____ matter.

3 Binta looks at two different soils.

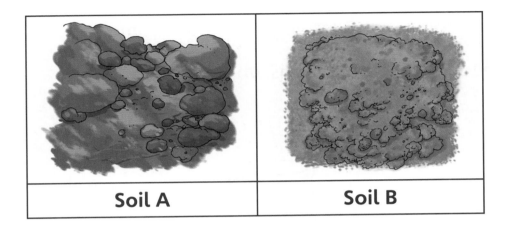

| Soil A | Soil B |

a) Describe **two** ways in which **Soil A** differs from **Soil B**.

1. _____

2. _____

b) Name **one** piece of equipment she could use to look more closely at the soils.

_____

c) (i) Binta sees this in one of the soils.

What is it?

_____

(ii) Name some other kinds of organic matter she may find in soil.

_____

_____

Different soils

1 Marco puts some water into a jar. He adds some soil.

When he looks at it later, this is what he sees.

Three layers are labelled.

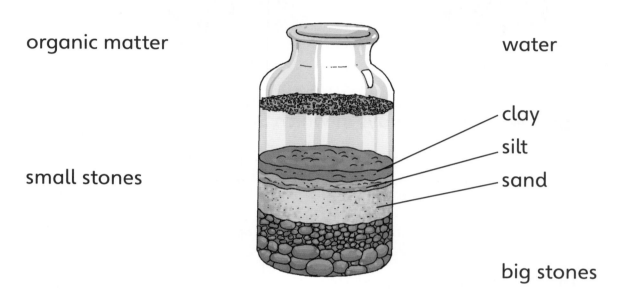

organic matter

small stones

water

clay

silt

sand

big stones

a) Complete the diagram by drawing the **four** missing label lines.

b) Draw **one** line from each layer to its description.

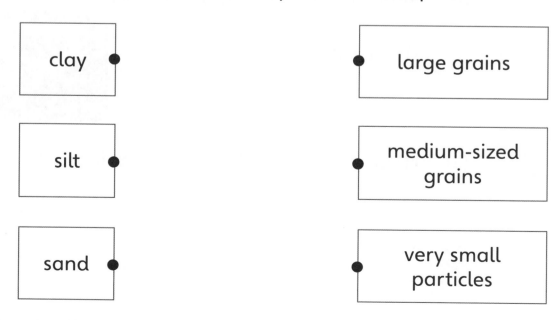

clay

silt

sand

large grains

medium-sized grains

very small particles

c)   Tick (✓) which of these are found in loam soil.

clay   ☐   silt   ☐   sand   ☐

d)   (i)   What is loam soil good for?

_____

(ii)   Give the reason that loam soil is good for this purpose.

_____

2   Complete the table for a soil you have looked at.

What colour is it?	
What does it feel like?	
Does it have stones in it?	
Can you see any organic matter? If so, what?	
Are there any large grains?	

Investigating soil

1 a) Write **sand** or **clay** under each diagram.

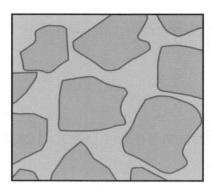 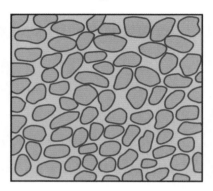

_____   _____

b) Which has larger air spaces? _____

c) Predict which will let more water run through it.

_____

2 Leah tests two soils to see how much water they let
through. She pours 100 cm³ water into each soil.

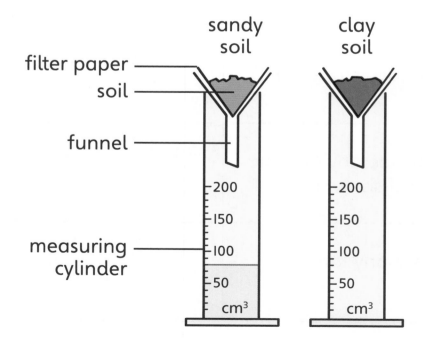

a) What types of soil is she using?

_____

b) (i) Name **one** piece of measuring equipment she uses.

_____

(ii) How much water goes through the sandy soil?

_____ cm³

(iii) **40 cm³** of water goes through the clay soil.

Show this by drawing it on the diagram.

c) (i) Which soil lets more water through?

_____

(ii) How did you decide which let more water through?

_____

d) Leah holds some of the wet clay soil and squeezes it.

Predict what happens when she squeezes the clay soil.

_____

Key to soils

1. Use the key to name each soil under its picture.

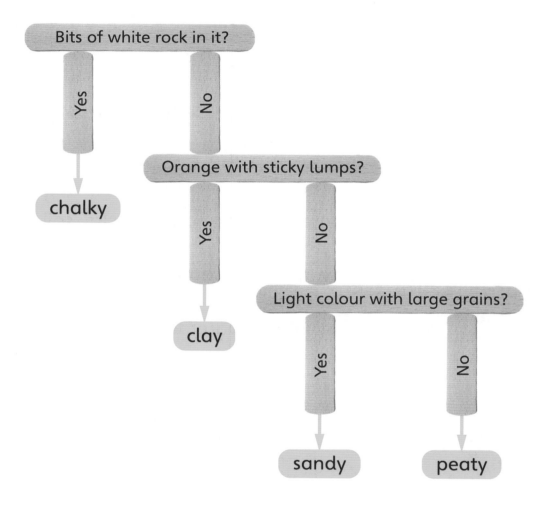

Bits of white rock in it?

Yes → chalky

No → Orange with sticky lumps?

Yes → clay

No → Light colour with large grains?

Yes → sandy

No → peaty

2 Use information from the key to describe each soil.

Picture of soil	Description of soil
	_____ _____ _____ _____
	_____ _____ _____ _____
	_____ _____ _____ _____
	_____ _____ _____ _____

What have I learned?

1 I understand that different rocks have different properties and features. I can compare these for different rocks.

I know this because I can describe **one** feature of these rocks.

Pumice: _____

Granite: _____

2 I can identify different rocks by observing them, by using a key and by finding things out for myself.

I know this because I can identify these rocks.

_____   _____   _____

3 I can describe how sedimentary, igneous and metamorphic rocks are formed and how this affects whether they have fossils in them.

I know this because I can complete these sentences.

Sedimentary rock is made from _____ of

_____ that have been compacted.

Igneous rock is formed from _____ that

has _____ quickly or _____.

Metamorphic rock is formed when _____

rock or _____ rock is changed by heat and

_____.

Fossils are usually found in _____ rock.

4 I can explain how rocks can be broken down into smaller
pieces over time in different ways.

This can happen by a process called _____.

5 I understand that soil contains small parts of rock and

_____ matter.

I can observe and compare features of soils such as colour,
texture and how well water drains through them.

I know this because I can write **one** way in which sandy soil
differs from clay soil.

_____

6 I can identify different soils by observing them, by using a
key and by finding things out for myself.

I know this because I can use the soil key in my textbook and
name places where I can find things out for myself.

I can find things out in these places: _____

_____

Using and changing materials

Materials have different properties. Some materials change when they are heated. Some materials change when they are cooled. Some materials can be changed by twisting, squashing, bending or squeezing.

In this unit we will learn:

- how to compare a range of materials with different properties

- to describe how objects made of some materials can be changed by squashing, bending, twisting and squeezing

- that some objects can be changed by the above actions but cannot be changed back easily

- that some materials change when they are heated or cooled and that this can change their properties

- the difference between the terms 'melting', 'freezing', 'evaporating' and 'condensing'.

Do you eat ice cream on a hot day? We store ice cream in a freezer to keep it cold. Suggest what starts to happen to the ice cream when we take it out of the freezer.

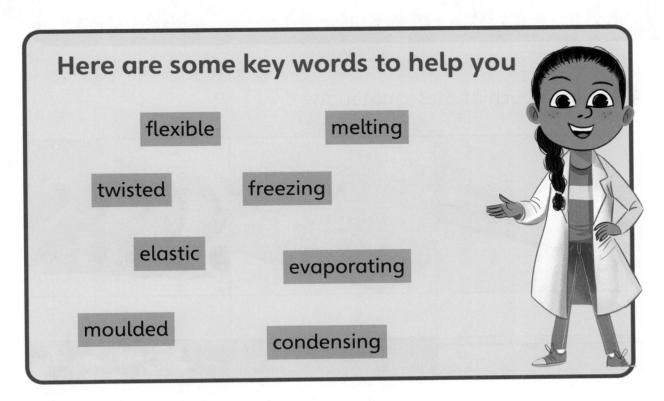

Here are some key words to help you

flexible   melting

twisted   freezing

elastic

evaporating

moulded

condensing

Choose two key words from the box above.
Write or draw what they mean.

More materials

1 Name each of these materials.

2 Name **one** object that can be made from each material.

Material	Object made from it
wood	
plastic	
cotton	
stone	

3 Look at some materials.

Complete the table with your observations.

Describe each material using these words.

hard   flexible   soft   waterproof

absorbent   rough   dull   shiny   smooth

Material	Words to describe it	What happens when water is dripped onto it?

Changing shape

1 a) Draw **one** line from each object to the material it is made of.

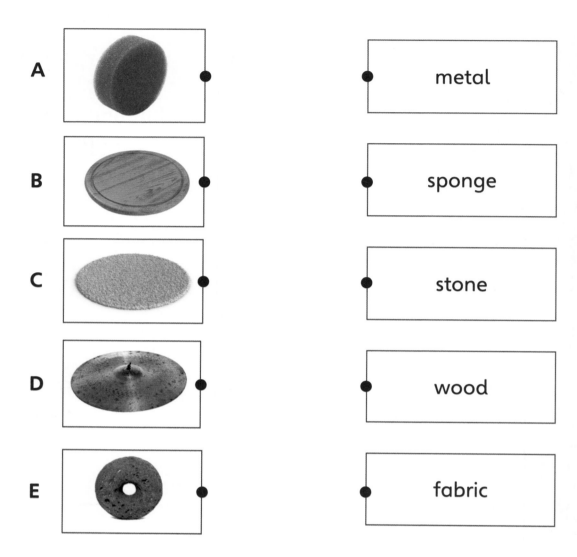

A

B

C

D

E

metal

sponge

stone

wood

fabric

b) (i) Which **two** letters show objects that are easy to bend?

_____ and _____

(ii) Which object can be squeezed most easily?

_____

2 Test some objects made of different materials to see if you can squeeze, bend or twist them.

a) Put a tick (✓) or a cross (✗) to show your results.

Name of object	Can it be squeezed?	Can it be bent?	Can it be twisted?

b) (i) Which materials are easy to bend, twist or squeeze?

_____

(ii) Which materials are harder to bend, twist or squeeze?

_____

1 Draw a line from each object to show whether it is being **squeezed** or **stretched**.

squeezed

stretched

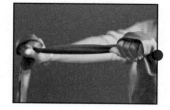

2   Test some objects made of different materials to see if you can squeeze or stretch them.

a)   Write **Yes** or **No** to show your results.

Name of object	Squeezing		Stretching	
	Can it be squeezed?	Does it go back to its first shape?	Can it be stretched?	Does it go back to its first shape?

b)   Are any of your objects elastic? Which?

_____

c)   Which object was easiest to:

(i)   squeeze? _____

(ii)   stretch? _____

No going back

1 a) What is the person doing to this plastic bottle?

_____

b) Will it go back to its first shape?

_____

c) What is the person doing to this rubber band? _____

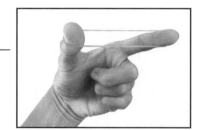

d) Write **one** property of the rubber band that makes it go back to its first shape. _____

2 The boy blows into a balloon.

a) Circle the word that describes what is happening to the balloon.

stretching   squashing

squeezing   twisting

b) Predict what will happen if the boy keeps blowing into the balloon for a long time.

_____

3 a) Write **one** word to describe this can.

_____

b) What material is it made from?

_____

4 a) Circle what you think someone tried to do to this stick.

squeeze   bend

squash   stretch

b) (i) What has happened to the stick?

_____

(ii) Will it go back to its first shape? _____

c) Describe what has happened to this football.

Include similar things to those you wrote about the stick.

_____

_____

_____

_____

Looking at clay

1 a) Circle the object made of clay.

b) Complete the sentence.

Clay is made from _____ particles of

_____.

c) Write **two** words to describe what someone is doing to this material.

1. _____   2. _____

2 a) What material is each roof made of? Write under the pictures.

b) Circle **two** words that describe **both** roof materials.

soft   stiff   elastic   hard   absorbent

3 The pictures show people with clay.

Write one or two sentences next to each picture to describe what they are doing.

_____

_____

_____

_____

_____

_____

_____

_____

_____

_____

_____

_____

_____

_____

_____

_____

Heating and cooling

1 Put a **red** cross next to all the objects used to **heat** things.

Draw a **blue** circle around all the objects used to **cool** things.

2 a) (i) What is the yellow and orange material in this picture?

_____

(ii) What is this material coming out of?

_____

(iii) What happens to this material when it cools?

_____

b) Describe this molten metal.

_____

_____

c) What will this metal be like when it is cool again?

_____

3 Draw a bar of chocolate that has been heated and when it has been cooled again.

Heated	Cooled

Melting and freezing

1. Natsuko puts ice cubes in her drink on a hot day.

   a) Circle the place where she keeps ice cubes.

   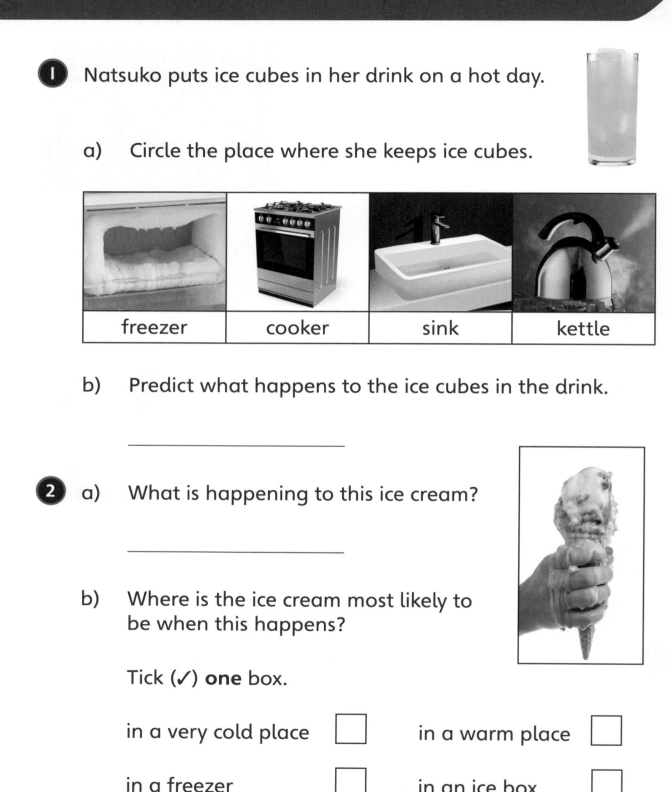

   | freezer | cooker | sink | kettle |

   b) Predict what happens to the ice cubes in the drink.

   _____

2. a) What is happening to this ice cream?

   _____

   b) Where is the ice cream most likely to be when this happens?

   Tick (✓) **one** box.

   in a very cold place ☐   in a warm place ☐

   in a freezer ☐   in an ice box ☐

3 Mika is making ice cubes.

What must he do to the water to make ice cubes?

Tick (✓) **one** box.

heat it ☐   cover it ☐

melt it ☐   freeze it ☐

4 The pictures show an ice cube and some cold butter.

Draw what they look like when they get warmer.

Cold	Warmer
ice cube	
butter	

Evaporating and condensing

1 Use label lines and words to label **ice** and **water** in this Arctic habitat.

2 **a)** What is happening to the water in this kettle?

Tick (✓) **one** box.

it is evaporating ☐   it is freezing ☐

it is melting ☐   it is cooling ☐

b) What is happening to the water **on the lid**?

Tick (✓) **two** boxes.

it is getting hot ☐

it is condensing ☐

it is cooling ☐

it is melting ☐

it is freezing ☐

lid

3 Write a number or a letter from the diagram to answer the questions about water.

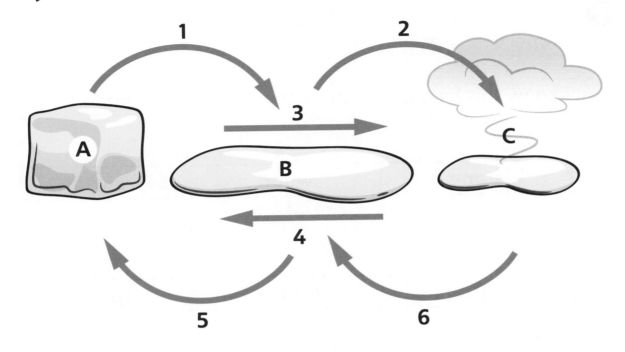

a) (i) Which **letter** shows **ice**? _____

(ii) Which **letter** shows **water vapour**? _____

b) (i) Which **number** shows **heating**? _____

(ii) Which **number** shows **cooling**? _____

c) (i) Which **number** shows **melting**? _____

(ii) Which **number** shows **freezing**? _____

d) (i) Which **number** shows **evaporating**? _____

(ii) Which **number** shows **condensing**? _____

What have I learned?

1 I can compare a range of materials with different properties.

I know this because I can write a word to describe each of these materials.

stone	wood	plastic
cotton	rubber	sponge

2 I can describe how objects made of some materials can be changed by squashing, bending, twisting and squeezing.

I understand that some objects can be changed by the above actions but cannot be changed back easily.

I know this because I can write a word to describe what has happened to each of these objects.

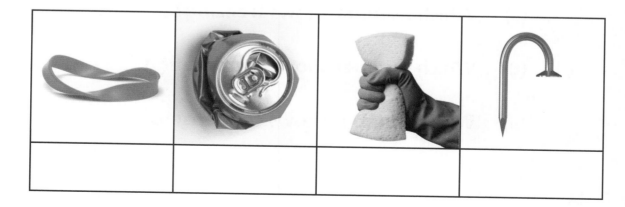

3 I understand that some materials can change when they are heated and/or cooled and that this can change their properties.

I know this because I can describe what happens to metal and to chocolate when they are heated and then cooled.

Metal _____

_____

_____

Chocolate _____

_____

_____

4 I understand the difference between the terms **melting**, **freezing**, **evaporating** and **condensing**.

I know this because I can write one of these terms under each picture.

Light

We need light to be able to see things. Darkness is the absence of light. Sources of light help us to see things in the world around us. Some objects reflect light. Some materials block light.

In this unit we will learn:

- that we need light to be able to see things

- that darkness is the absence of light

- that light comes from a source

- that, although some objects can reflect light, they are not sources of light

- that some materials block light and are opaque

- that opaque objects blocking light can form shadows

- about patterns in the way that the sizes of shadows change

- the difference between the terms 'transparent', 'translucent' and 'opaque'.

There are many light sources in space. Stars like our Sun are sources of light. The Moon reflects the Sun's light. What light sources do you have in your home? Can you see any objects nearby that reflect light?

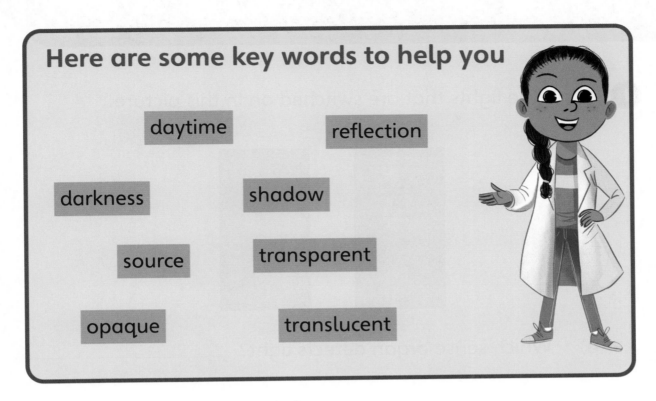

Here are some key words to help you

daytime

reflection

darkness

shadow

source

transparent

opaque

translucent

Choose two key words from the box above.
Write or draw what they mean.

What is darkness?

1 Circle the lights that are switched on in this picture.

a)   Which sense organ detects light? _____

b)   What do we need light to help us to do?

_____

c)   Where does most of our light come from in daytime?

_____

2 The picture shows a house at night.

Write **two** things that show it is night.

1.   _____

2.   _____

3 Some green plants are growing in just one place in this cave.

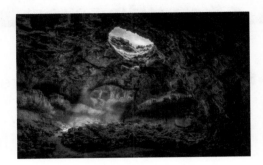

a) Does this picture show daytime or night?
Tick (✔) **one** box.

daytime ☐   night ☐

Write **one** thing you can see that tells you this.

_____

_____

b) Why is it dark inside the cave?

_____

c) Suggest why the green plants only grow in one place.

_____

d) Name **one** piece of equipment that you need to be able to see inside a cave.

_____

e) Complete the sentence to describe the light in a cave.

The further you go into the cave, the

_____ it gets.

Sources of light

1. This picture shows fireworks in the sky over some buildings.

    a) Is it daytime or night?

    _____

    b) Write **two** sources of light you can see in the picture.

    1. _____

    2. _____

    c) Which part of the picture is dark? _____

    d) Name **two** sense organs that can tell you a firework is in the sky.

    1. _____   2. _____

    e) Predict what the sky looks like when the fireworks stop.

    _____

2. a) What is the source of light for Earth? _____

    b) Why is it **not** safe to look at this light source?

    _____

3 Draw some light sources you see in these places.

Light sources inside your home or school

Light sources outdoors

Reflecting light

1 Circle **sources** of light in **red**.

Draw a **blue** line under things that **reflect** light.

2 This tape reflects light.
People put it on clothes and other objects.

a) Suggest why these workers have the tape on their clothes.

_____

_____

b) The person taking this picture has a light source.

Discuss the picture with a partner.

- What does the picture show?

- Why can you **not** see the colour of the people's clothes?

- How do you know there must be a light source?

- What would the picture look like if the light source was switched off?

Opaque objects

1 The picture shows a shadow on a screen.

a) (i) Label these things on the picture using a line and the word each time.

screen   torch   toy bear   shadow

(ii) On the list above circle **two** things that are the same shape.

b) In the picture, which object is a light source?

_____

c) (i) What is the scientific name for an object that

blocks light? _____

(ii) In the picture, which object blocks light?

_____

d) What happens to the shadow when the torch is switched off?

_____

2 a) Name the light source in this picture.

_____

b) Name the object blocking the light.

_____

3 Suggest what is blocking the light in each picture below.

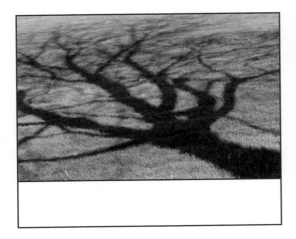

Shadows

1 Draw **one** line from each animal to its shadow.

2 Huma makes the shadow of a football on a wall.

a) Draw a football in the correct place to make this shadow.

b) Name the light source here. _____

c)   Circle **all** the objects that will make a shadow with the
      same shape as the football.

d)   What does the word *opaque* mean?

_____

e)   Draw the shape of the shadow for each of these
      objects.

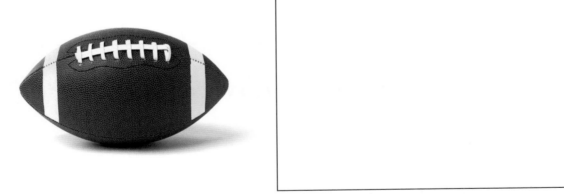

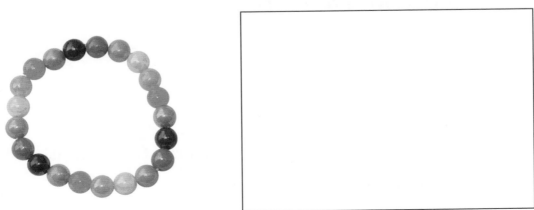

Shadow sizes

Do the investigation about shadow heights in your textbook to answer this scientific question:

How does the [position of the light source] ◄——— change this

affect the [height of the shadow?] ◄——— measure this

1 a) Name the measuring equipment you need.

_____

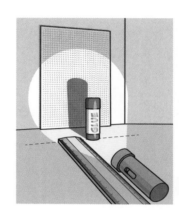

b) What is your light source?

_____

c) (i) Write **one** thing you will change.

_____

(ii) Write **one** thing you will measure.

_____

(iii) Write **one** thing you will **keep the same** each time.

_____

d) Complete this prediction.

As the torch moves further from the glue stick, I think

the height of the shadow will be _____.

2 a) Write the second column heading for the results table.

Distance of light source from the glue stick in cm	

b) Write your results in the table.

c) Complete this sentence to describe the pattern in your results.

As the torch moves further from the glue stick,

the _____ of the shadow gets

_____.

d) What could you do about any results that do not fit the pattern?

_____

e) Can you think of any ways to improve your investigation?

_____

_____

Opaque, transparent and translucent

1 Circle all the opaque objects.

2 Bathroom windows often have glass like this.

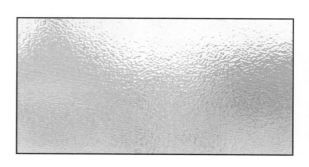

a) Write **one** word to describe this glass.

_____

b) Why is this glass good for bathroom windows?

_____

_____

_____

3 a) Draw **one** line from each container to a scientific term that describes it.

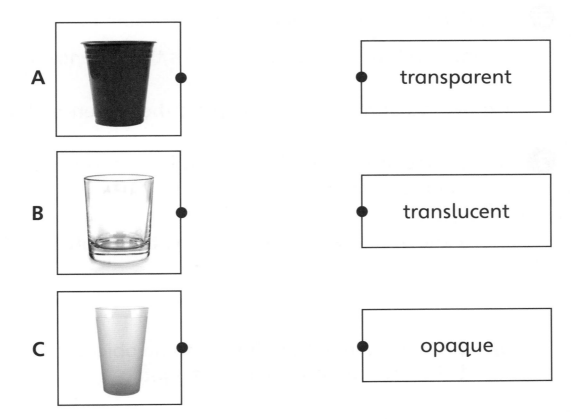

A   transparent

B   translucent

C   opaque

b) Which container can you see things through very clearly?

_____

c) Which letter shows the container that will make the **darkest** shadow?

_____

d) Which letter shows the container that only lets some light through it?

_____

What have I learned?

1 I understand that we need light to be able to _____

things and that _____ is the absence of light.

I know this because I can complete the sentence above.

2 a) I understand that light comes from a source and know some sources of light.

I know this because I can name **two** sources of light.

1. _____ 2. _____

b) I can explain that, although some objects can reflect light, they are **not** sources of light.

I know this because I can name **two** objects that reflect light but are **not** light sources.

1. _____ 2. _____

3 I understand that some materials block light and are described as being opaque.

I can circle **two** opaque objects.

4 I understand that when light from a source is blocked by an opaque object, a shadow can form that is the same shape as the object.

I can draw the shape of the shadow that these objects make.

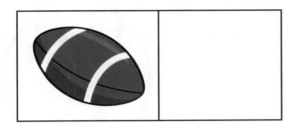

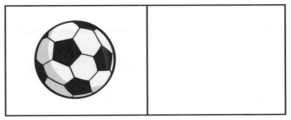

5 I understand patterns in the way that the sizes of shadows change.

I can complete this sentence.

The closer the light source to the object the _____

the shadow will be.

6 I know the difference between the terms **transparent**, **translucent** and **opaque**.

I know this because I can write one of those terms under each picture.

Forces and friction

Forces make objects move. Friction is a force that slows things down. Sometimes friction can be helpful. It helps us to write without the pencil slipping. Sports teams that want to be faster may work to reduce friction as much as they can.

In this unit we will learn:

- that a force is needed to make objects move
- how to describe and compare how objects move on different surfaces and slopes
- to describe friction as a contact force that acts between surfaces to slow down movement
- to describe some ways in which friction between solid surfaces can be increased or decreased.

Pushes and pulls are forces that make objects move. Friction is a force that slows down movement. Think about the surface of a water slide. Why do slides need to be so smooth?

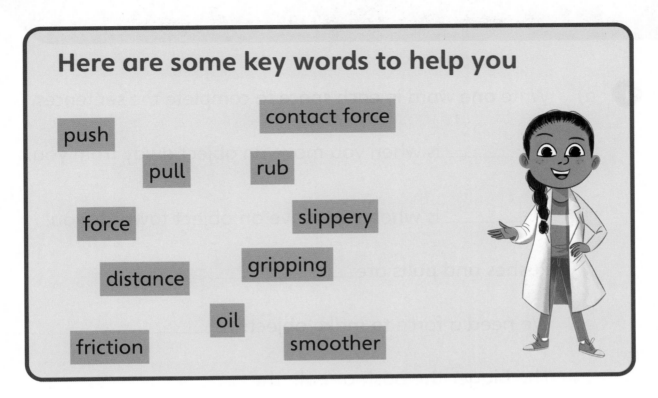

Here are some key words to help you

push

pull

contact force

rub

force

slippery

distance

gripping

oil

friction

smoother

Choose two key words from the box above.
Write or draw what they mean.

Forces that make things move

1 a) Write **one** word in each space to complete the sentences.

A _____ is when you move an object away from you.

A _____ is when you move an object towards you.

Pushes and pulls are _____.

We need a force to make objects _____.

The bigger the push or pull, the _____ the force.

b) Draw a picture of a person who is:

(i) **pulling** an object

(ii) **pushing** an object

2 Try pushing a toy car or other small object.

a) Make a start line to use every time.
Why do you need to do this?

_____

b) Give the car a small push. Measure how far it moves.
Write the *number* in the results table.

The unit
is already
here.

Size of push	Distance car moves in cm
small	
medium	
big	

c) Now give the car a medium push and then a big push.

(i) Complete the results table.

(ii) Complete the conclusion below.

The _____ the push, the

_____ the car moves.

d) Look at someone else's results.

(i) Is their **pattern** the same as yours? _____

(ii) Are their **distances** the same as yours? _____

Suggest a reason for this.

_____

Moving on different surfaces

1 Think of some surfaces that are rough and some surfaces that are smooth.

Write or draw them in the circles.

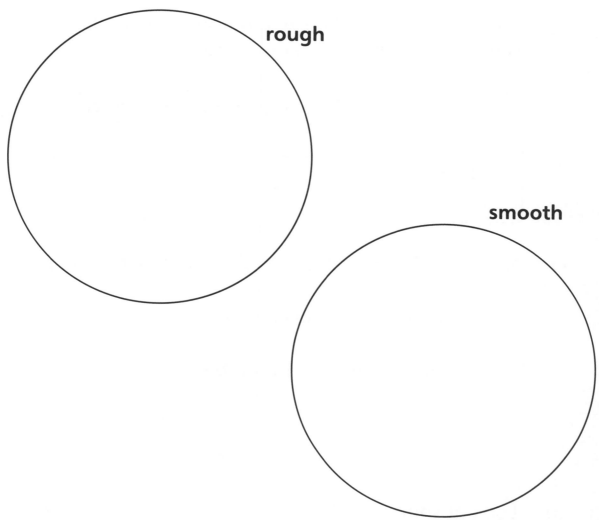

rough

smooth

2 Investigate how a toy car moves on different surfaces.

a) Complete the scientific question.

How does the smoothness of a surface affect the

_____ the car moves?

b) (i) Write the correct column headings in the results table.

(ii) Write your results in the table.

c) Which was the smoothest surface you tested?

_____

d) Which was the roughest surface you tested?

_____

e) Complete the sentence about your results.

The smoother the surface, the _____ the car moves.

f) Were there any results that did **not** fit the pattern?

_____

Improving an investigation

1 What does the word *improve* mean?

_____

2 Think about your investigation with the car moving on different surfaces.

a) What **one** thing did you [change] in the investigation?

_____

b) What **one** thing did you [measure] ?

_____

c) What measuring equipment did you use?

_____

d) What did you keep the same to make it a fair test? Write **two** different things.

1. _____

2. _____

e) How did you make the car's **start** the same for each surface?

_____

_____

f) How did you make the car's **finish line** the same for each surface?

_____

_____

g) Which thing did you find hardest to keep the same?

_____

h) Can you think of a better way of doing it now?

_____

_____

3 Asha suggests starting the car on a slope instead of pushing it.

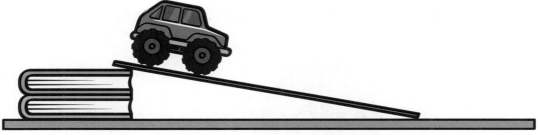

a) Suggest why pushing the car is **not** a fair start.

_____

b) Why would starting the car on a slope be fairer?

_____

Friction

1 a) Complete the sentences.

Pushes and pulls are _____ that can make objects start to move.

b) What does friction do to moving objects?

_____

c) Circle the **two** answers that describe friction.

easy to see   absorbent   transparent

invisible   a contact force

d) This car is moving along a road.

The **red** arrow shows where friction acts.

(i) Draw an arrow to show another place where friction acts.

(ii) What does friction do to the car's movement?

_____

2 a) Name **one smooth** floor surface and **one rough** floor surface.

smooth: _____   rough: _____

b) Write **lots of friction** or **less friction** above the correct car.

_____   _____

car moving on
smooth floor

same car moving
on **rough** floor

c) Complete the sentence.

The rougher the surface, the _____ friction there is.

3 Rub your hands together.

a) Which force acts between your moving hands?

_____

b) Press your hands together as you rub.
What difference does pressing them together make?

_____

c) Complete the sentence.

The more the surfaces press together, the

_____ friction there is.

Increasing friction

1 a) Tick (✓) the correct meaning of the word *increase*.

to make something **smaller** ☐

to keep something the **same size** ☐

to make something **bigger** ☐

b) (i) Increase the number of sweets in this pile.

(ii) Increase the size of this lolly.

2 Complete the sentences about friction.

Friction is a _____ that acts between two surfaces.

One way to increase friction is to make one or both surfaces

_____.

3 Describe what you can see in each picture and how it **increases** friction.

_____

_____

_____

_____

_____

_____

_____

_____

_____

_____

_____

_____

Reducing friction

1 a) Tick (✓) the correct meaning of the word *reduce*.

to make something **smaller** ☐

to keep something the **same size** ☐

to make something **bigger** ☐

b) Circle **one** word that also means reduce.

increase   rub   move   decrease   improve

2 Complete the sentences about reducing friction.

Friction is a force that acts between two

_____.

One way to reduce friction is to make one or both surfaces

_____.

The picture shows another way to reduce friction.

This person is putting _____

into a _____ engine.

The _____ flows between

the moving surfaces and reduces the

_____ between them.

3 Draw two pictures of people doing sports on very smooth surfaces, such as ice or snow.

Use your textbook for one and find out one by yourself.

1 I understand that a force is needed to make objects move.

I know this because I can draw something being pushed to make it move.

pushing

I can also draw something being pulled to make it move.

pulling

2 I can describe and compare how objects move on different surfaces and slopes.

I know this because I can predict how far the same toy car will move on different surfaces.

On a _____ surface the car will move a longer distance.

On a _____ surface the car will move a shorter distance.

3 I can describe friction as a contact force that acts between surfaces to slow down movement.

A contact force is a force that occurs when surfaces

_____ each other.

I can also show a place where friction acts on this moving car.

I can describe some ways in which friction between solid surfaces can be increased or decreased.

I know this because I can draw a car tyre to show how it is designed to increase friction.

I also know that when moving

surfaces, like my hands,

press together harder this

_____ friction between them.

I can also write **two** ways in which friction can be decreased or reduced.

1. Make the surfaces _____.

2. Put _____ between the moving surfaces.

Magnets

Magnetism is an invisible force. Magnets pull some materials towards them, but not others. A magnet can make a magnetic object move without touching it. Many explorers have relied on the magnet in their compass to point them North.

In this unit we will learn:

- that magnets have two poles, known as North and South

- the difference between the terms 'attract' and 'repel'

- to predict whether two magnets will attract or repel each other, depending on which poles are facing

- that some forces need contact between two objects, but magnetic forces can act at a distance

- to identify materials that are magnetic and those that are non-magnetic.

Have you seen magnetic letters or numbers that stick onto a fridge? Or magnets that hold cupboard doors closed?
A compass is a magnet.
Find out what it is used for.

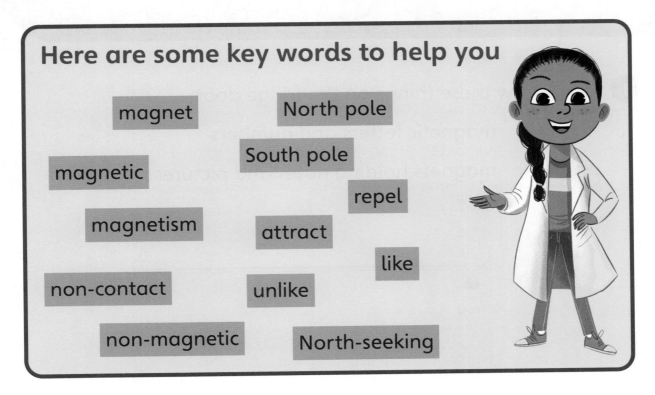

Here are some key words to help you

magnet

North pole

magnetic

South pole

repel

magnetism

attract

like

non-contact

unlike

non-magnetic

North-seeking

Choose two key words from the box above.
Write or draw what they mean.

Magnets

1 a) Draw these things on the fridge door:

- magnetic letters and numbers

- magnets holding notes and pictures.

b) Write **one** other way we can use magnets at home.

_____

2 Draw and name **four** other types of magnet that you might use at school.

Shape of magnet	Name of magnet

3 a) Magnetic forces are **non-contact** forces.
What does this mean?

_____

_____

b) Write **one** word that means *the force of a magnet*.

_____

Magnetic materials

1 a) Test some objects in your classroom to see if they are attracted to a magnet. Complete the table.

Object	Is it attracted to a magnet?

b) Circle **one** word from **each** box to describe the type of materials that are attracted to a magnet.

some
all

plastics   metals
fabrics

c) Name **two** magnetic materials.

1. _____   2. _____

2 Predict whether each of these objects will be magnetic or non-magnetic. Write each name in the correct circle.

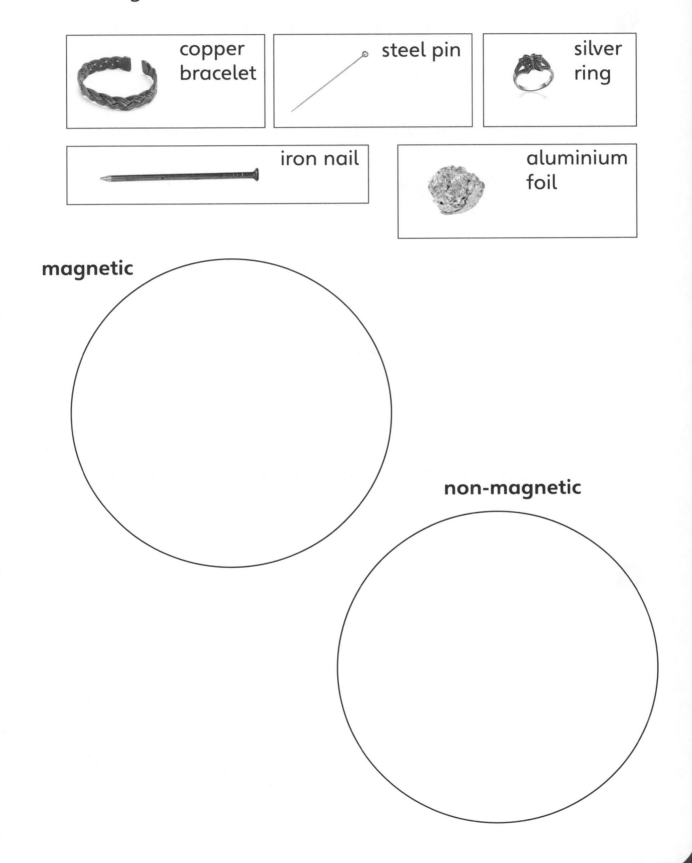

copper bracelet	
steel pin	
silver ring	
iron nail	
aluminium foil	

magnetic

non-magnetic

North and South

1 a) Circle **one** word to name the two ends of a magnet.

places   poles   parts   pieces

b) What do the letters **N** and **S** on a magnet mean?

N means _____.

S means _____.

c) (i) Colour the magnet in colours you usually see on magnets.

(ii) Write **N** and **S** on it in the correct places.

d) What name do we use for a magnet that is this shape?

_____

2 a) Colour this magnet and write **N** and **S** on it.

b) Write the name for a magnet that is this shape.

_____

3 a) (i) Write **N** and **S** on **both** ends of **every** magnet to show them **repelling** one another.

(ii) Draw **one arrow** under each of the **four magnets** to show the direction in which it moves to **repel** the other magnet.

b) What force causes the magnets to repel?

_____

c) How do we know this force is there if we cannot see it?

_____

_____

Attract and repel

1. Write the **two** missing letters on this bar magnet.

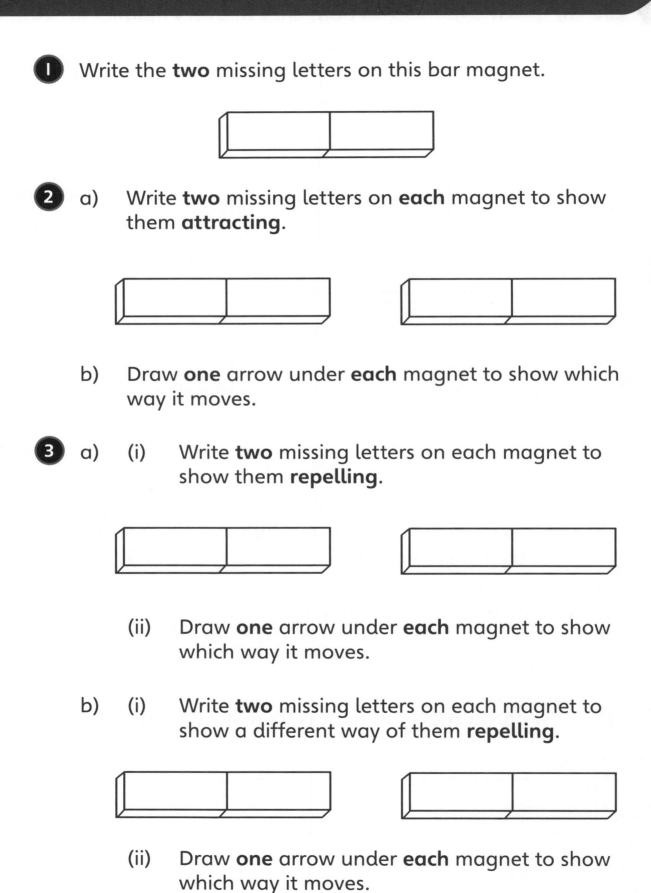

2. a) Write **two** missing letters on **each** magnet to show them **attracting**.

    b) Draw **one** arrow under **each** magnet to show which way it moves.

3. a) (i) Write **two** missing letters on each magnet to show them **repelling**.

        (ii) Draw **one** arrow under **each** magnet to show which way it moves.

    b) (i) Write **two** missing letters on each magnet to show a different way of them **repelling**.

        (ii) Draw **one** arrow under **each** magnet to show which way it moves.

4 Class 3 look at this equipment with their teacher.

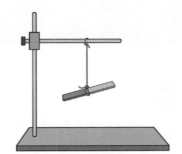

a) Describe how the magnet moves.

_____

b) The teacher brings another magnet close to the first one.

(i) What do the magnets do?

_____

(ii) Write all the missing letters on these magnets to show why this happens.

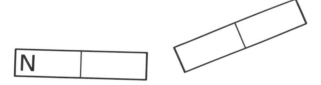

c) The teacher turns one magnet around.

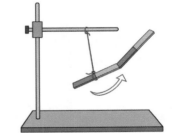

(i) What do the magnets do?

_____

(ii) Write all the missing letters on these magnets to show why this happens.

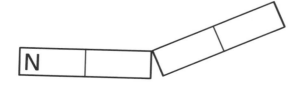

Fun things to try

1 a)   This magnet is close to some paperclips.

Finish the picture by drawing what happens to the paperclips.

b)   Your textbook shows how to make a chain of paperclips with a magnet.

Draw what happened when you did this.

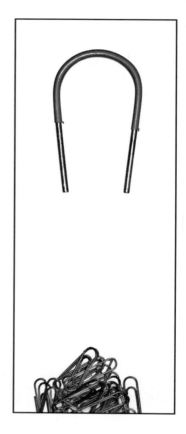

2 a) Name **two** metals that are magnetic.

1. _____

2. _____

b) The picture shows a magnet and some pins.

Complete the sentences.

The magnet _____ the pins.

The pins are sticking to the

_____ because they are

made of a _____ material.

3 Complete the rules for magnetic poles.

Like poles _____ .

Unlike poles _____ .

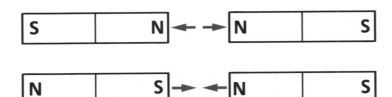

Which magnet is the strongest?

1 Test some magnets to see which is the strongest.
Draw all the magnets you use here.
Label each of them with a number.

2 a) Count how many paperclips each magnet can hold.
Complete the table with your results.

Magnet	How many paperclips does it hold?

b) Which magnet is the strongest in this test?

3 Test each magnet using this equipment.

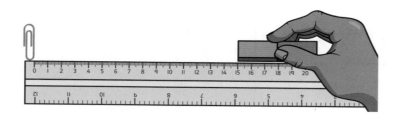

a) Write **two** things that you kept the same every time you did this test.

I. _____ 2. _____

b) Complete the results table.

Remember the unit is already here!

Magnet	Distance of magnet when paperclip moved in cm

c) (i) Which magnet is the strongest in this test? ☐

   (ii) How did you decide which magnet was the strongest?

   _____

4 a) Was the same magnet the strongest in both tests?

   _____

b) Do the results for the two tests put all the magnets in the same order of strength?

   _____

c) Write **one** thing you could improve in either of the tests.

   _____

What have I learned?

1 I can describe magnets as having two poles, known as North and South.

I can put their letters and colours on these magnets.

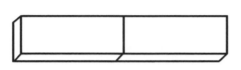 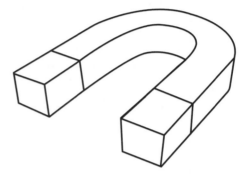

2 I know the difference between the terms 'attract' and 'repel'.

I can complete these rules:

Like poles _____.

Unlike poles _____.

3 I can predict whether two magnets will attract or repel each other, depending on which poles are facing.

I can write **attract** or **repel** next to each pair of magnets on the next page.

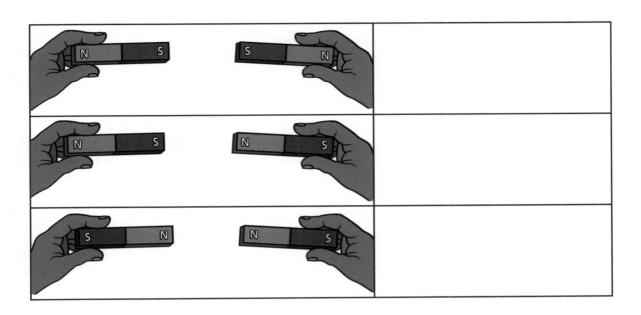

4 I understand that some forces need contact between two objects, but magnetic forces can act at a distance.

I know this because friction is a contact force, but

magnetism is a _____-_____ force.

5 I can identify materials that are magnetic and those that are non-magnetic.

I can apply this knowledge when I use magnets.

I know this because I can name **two metals** that are **magnetic**.

1. _____   2. _____

I can also name **two non-magnetic** materials.

1. _____   2. _____

My notes

My notes

My notes

My notes

(key: b-bottom, c-centre, l-left, r-right, t-top)